BONES
The Skeletal System

Gillian Houghton

Rosen
Classroom

New York

Published in 2007 by The Rosen Publishing Group, Inc.
29 East 21st Street, New York, NY 10010

First Edition

Editor: Amelie von Zumbusch
Book Design: Greg Tucker

Photo Credits: Cover © 3D4Medical.com/Getty Images; p. 5 © Dauenheimer/Custom Medical Stock Photo; p. 6 (left) © Michel Gilles/Photo Researchers, Inc.; p. 6 (right) © A. Hubrich/zefa/Corbis; p. 9 © Articulate Graphics/Custom Medical Stock Photo; p. 10 (left) © David Bassett/Photo Researchers, Inc.; p. 10 (right) © John M. Daugherty/Photo Researchers, Inc.; p. 13 (left) © Emely/zefa/Corbis; pp. 13 (right),14 (left),18 (left) © Anatomical Travelogue/Photo Researchers, Inc.; p. 14 (right) © Paul Barton/Corbis; p. 17 © Birmingham/Custom Medical Stock Photo; p. 18 (right) © C.Lyttle/zefa/Corbis; p. 21 (left) © Astrid & Hanns-Frieder Michler/Photo Researchers, Inc.; p. 21(right) © Herb Watson/Corbis.

Library of Congress Cataloging-in-Publication Data

Houghton, Gillian.
  Bones : the skeletal system / Gillian Houghton.— 1st ed.
    p. cm. — (Body works)
  Includes index.
  ISBN (10) 1-4042-3473-X (13) 978-1-4042-3473-4 (library binding) — ISBN (10) 1-4042-2182-4 (13) 978-1-4042-2182-6 (pbk.)
  1. Human skeleton—Juvenile literature. I. Title. II. Series.
  QM101.H74 2007
  611'.71—dc22
                                2005037488

Manufactured in the United States of America

CPSIA Compliance Information: Batch #CR516130RC: For further information contact Rosen Publishing, New York, New York at 1-800-237-9932.

Contents

The Skeletal System   4

Inside Bones   7

The Parts of a Joint   8

Kinds of Joints   11

The Bones of the Head   12

The Vertebral Column   15

The Rib Cage   16

The Shoulder, Arm, and Hand   19

The Hip, Leg, and Foot   20

Skeletal Problems   22

Glossary   23

Index   24

Web Sites   24

The Skeletal System

The skeletal system is made up of 206 bones that **support** the body. Bones **protect** the soft **tissues** and **organs** of the head and chest. More than 400 skeletal **muscles** are attached, or joined, to the bones. When skeletal muscles contract, or press together, the attached bones move.

When our bones and muscles work together, we can take a walk or play a game. We can pick up a book and flip through its pages. Bones help us to play, to work, and to learn about the world around us.

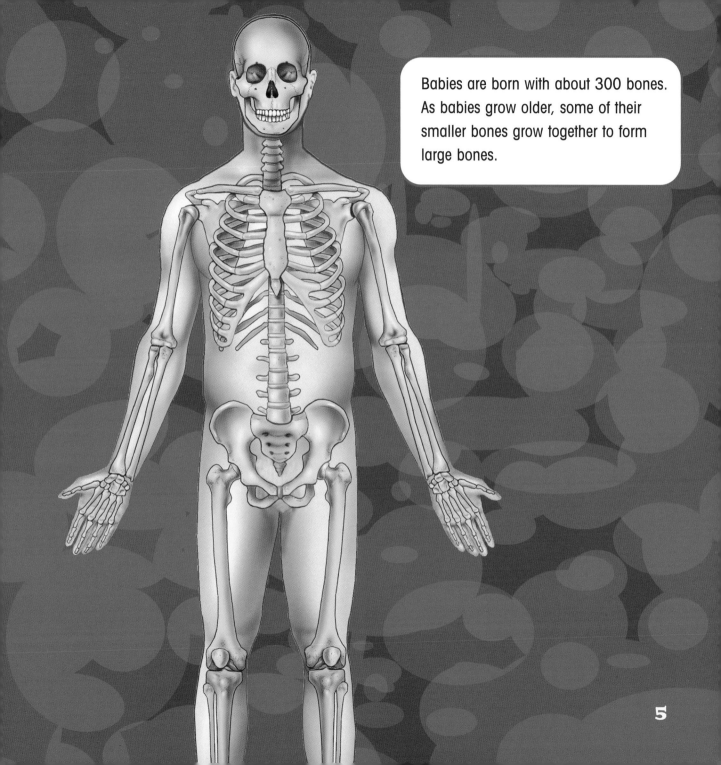

Babies are born with about 300 bones. As babies grow older, some of their smaller bones grow together to form large bones.

You need bones to walk, run, or kick a ball. *Inset:* The red pockets in this bone are bone marrow.

Inside Bones

The **skeletons** you have seen might look dry and easily broken, but the living bones in a person's body are strong. Living bones have a hard outside layer and a soft, lightweight center. The bone's soft center is called spongy bone. The hard outer tissue is bathed in blood and other **fluids**.

There is soft matter called bone marrow in the pockets of spongy bone. Bone marrow is also found in the center of the long arm and leg bones. Bone marrow stores fat and makes one kind of blood cell.

The Parts of a Joint

The place where two or more bones meet is called a joint. Smooth tissue called cartilage covers the ends of bones. Cartilage cushions, or softens, the movement of bones as they rub against one another. Without cartilage the ends of the bones would wear down and break.

Thin **membranes** are also attached to the bones. One type of membrane found between bones is called a joint capsule. Inside the joint capsule is the synovial membrane. This membrane makes a fluid that keeps cartilage smooth and stops it from drying out.

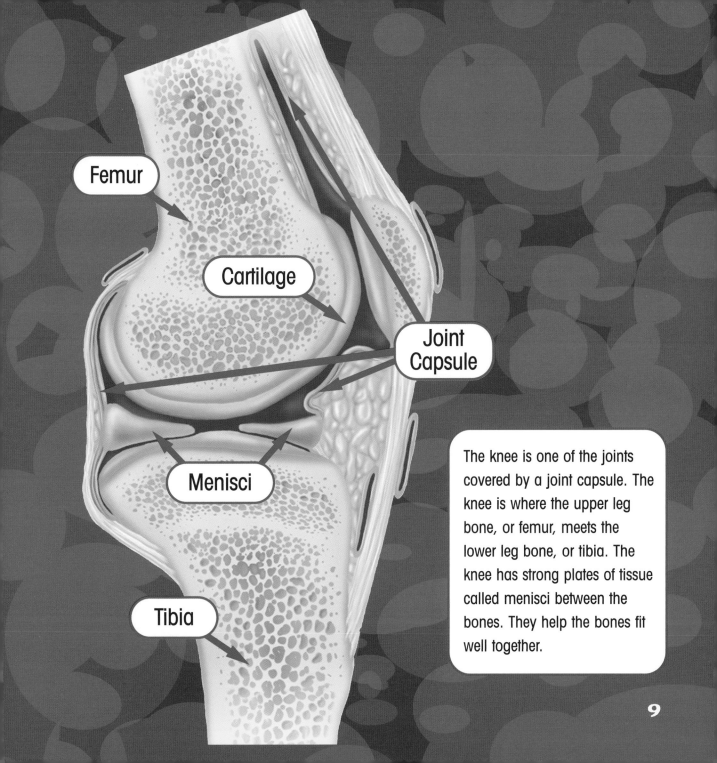

Femur

Cartilage

Joint Capsule

Menisci

Tibia

The knee is one of the joints covered by a joint capsule. The knee is where the upper leg bone, or femur, meets the lower leg bone, or tibia. The knee has strong plates of tissue called menisci between the bones. They help the bones fit well together.

9

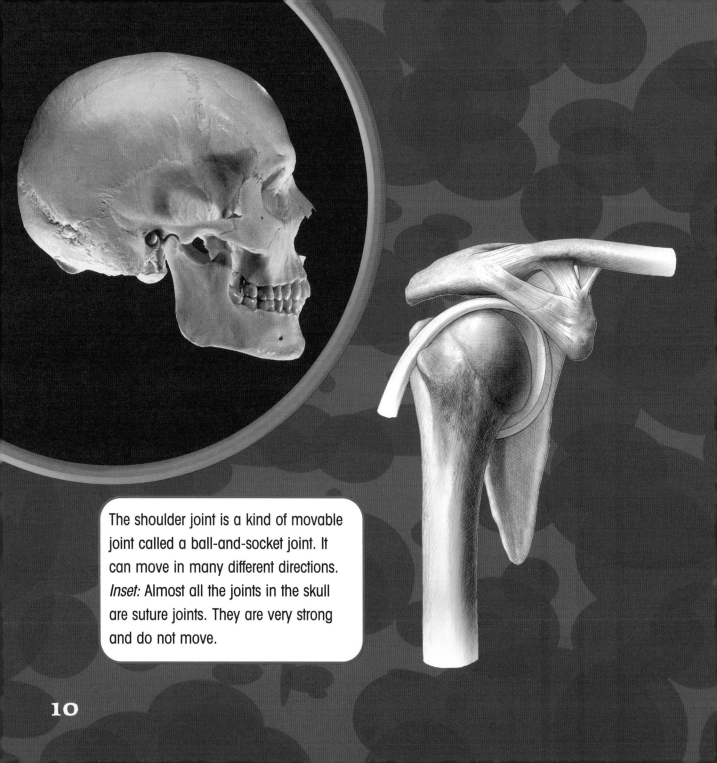

The shoulder joint is a kind of movable joint called a ball-and-socket joint. It can move in many different directions. *Inset:* Almost all the joints in the skull are suture joints. They are very strong and do not move.

Kinds of Joints

Your body has several kinds of joints. Each kind of joint allows a different amount of **flexibility**. A suture is a joint that allows no movement. Bones that meet in suture joints have uneven edges that fit together like puzzle pieces. Most of the bones of the **skull** are sutured together.

Slightly movable joints allow only certain movements. However, they are very strong. The **vertebral column** is made up of slightly movable joints. Most joints are movable joints. They allow much movement. Saddle joints and hinge joints are two common movable joints.

The Bones of the Head

The human skull has 28 bones. Except for the bottom **jaw** and the bones in the ears, all these bones are joined together and do not move. This makes the skull very strong. The skull must be strong to protect the **brain** and the **sense organs**.

The eight cranial bones form the rounded part of the skull, which covers the brain. The 14 facial bones give shape to the face. They make cavities, or openings, for the sense organs. They also shape the openings through which air, food, and water enter the body.

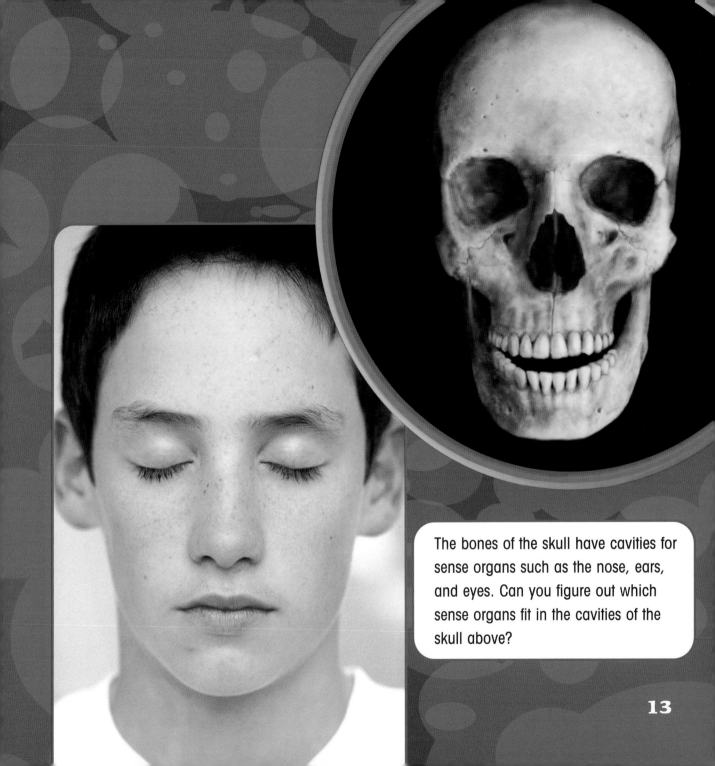

The bones of the skull have cavities for sense organs such as the nose, ears, and eyes. Can you figure out which sense organs fit in the cavities of the skull above?

13

The slightly movable joints of the vertebral column are very strong, but they also move enough for you to bend your back. *Inset:* You can see the spinal cord running through these four vertebrae.

The Vertebral Column

The vertebral column is a line of bones called vertebrae. It runs from the skull to the pelvis, or hip. At the center of each of the vertebrae is a hole. These holes form a tunnel called the spinal canal.

A line of **nerve** tissue called the spinal cord runs through the spinal canal. The spinal cord carries messages from every part of the body to the brain. The spinal cord also carries directions from the brain to the muscles. These directions let the muscles move the bones attached to them.

The Rib Cage

Joined to the vertebral column in the back are 12 pairs of flat bones called ribs. Flexible cartilage ties the top seven pairs of ribs to a bone called the sternum in the front. This lets the chest cavity grow larger and smaller as you breathe.

The ribs and the cartilage form the rib cage. The rib cage protects the organs, such as the heart, that lie within it. It also gives support to the shoulder **girdle**, which holds the arms in place.

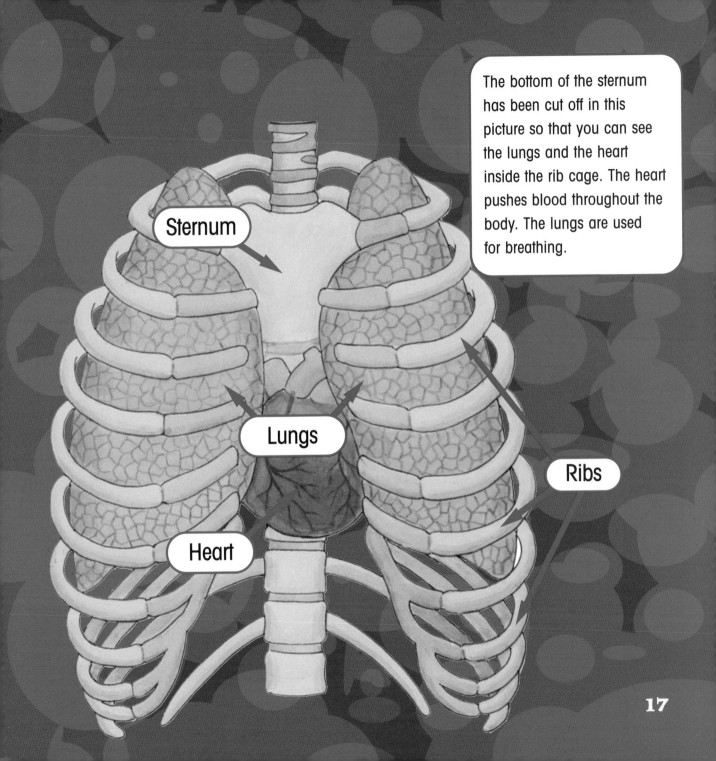

The bottom of the sternum has been cut off in this picture so that you can see the lungs and the heart inside the rib cage. The heart pushes blood throughout the body. The lungs are used for breathing.

Sternum

Lungs

Ribs

Heart

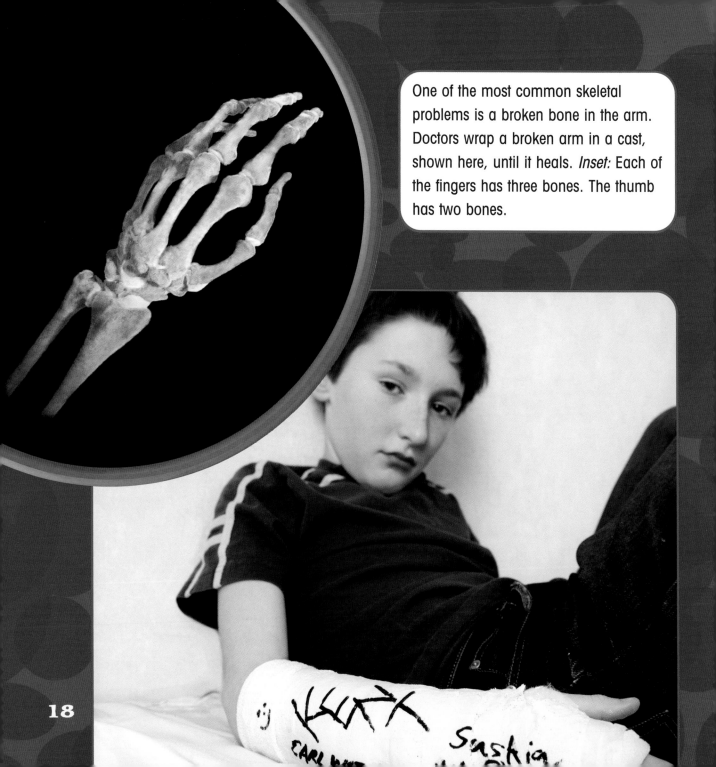

One of the most common skeletal problems is a broken bone in the arm. Doctors wrap a broken arm in a cast, shown here, until it heals. *Inset:* Each of the fingers has three bones. The thumb has two bones.

The Shoulder, Arm, and Hand

Both of the arms are attached to the shoulder girdle. The top bone of the arm is the humerus. It meets the shoulder girdle in a flexible ball-and-socket joint. The humerus meets the bones of the lower arm in a hinge joint called the elbow.

There are 27 bones in the wrist, hand, and fingers. The carpus bones make up the wrist, which joins the arm to the hand. The metacarpus bones make up the hand's wide pad. The fingers are made of bones called phalanges.

The Hip, Leg, and Foot

Just as the shoulder girdle holds the arms in place, the pelvic girdle holds the legs in place. The pelvic girdle is formed by two hip bones. On the outer side of each hip bone is a large opening. The rounded end of the femur fits into this opening and forms the hip joint. The femur is a large bone in the upper leg.

The femur meets the tibia and the fibula at the knee. The tibia and fibula make up the lower leg. They are attached to some of the 26 bones in the foot.

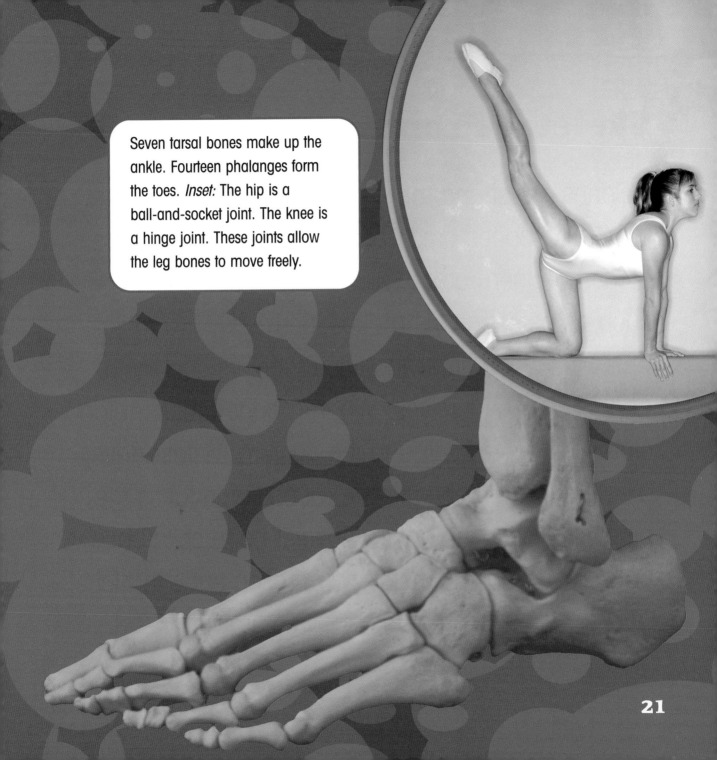

Seven tarsal bones make up the
ankle. Fourteen phalanges form
the toes. *Inset:* The hip is a
ball-and-socket joint. The knee is
a hinge joint. These joints allow
the leg bones to move freely.

Skeletal Problems

Bones are strong, but they sometimes break. Generally, bones break because too much force is placed on them or because a bone-related illness such as osteoporosis makes them easy to break.

Because they are living tissue, bones can mend and rebuild themselves. When a bone breaks, blood clots, or hardens, around the fracture. Within days, a callus, or hardened tissue, of cartilage takes the place of the clotted blood. Special bone cells build bone tissue that holds the two broken ends in place. Over the next few months, the fracture will mend.

Glossary

brain (BRAYN) The soft body part found in the head, which allows thought, movement, and feeling.

flexibility (flek-sih-BIH-lih-tee) An ability to move and bend in many directions.

fluids (FLOO-idz) Matter that moves like water.

girdle (GUR-dul) The bones that hold and support the arms or legs.

jaw (JAH) Bones in the top and bottom of the mouth.

membranes (MEM-braynz) Soft, thin pieces of living matter in a plant or an animal.

muscles (MUH-sulz) Parts of the body that are used to make the body move.

nerve (NERV) Having to do with the cells that carry messages between the brain and other parts of the body.

organs (OR-genz) The parts inside the body that do a job.

protect (pruh-TEKT) To keep from hurt.

sense organs (SENS OR-genz) Body parts that help the brain understand things about the world.

skeletons (SKEH-lih-tunz) The bones in an animal's or a person's body.

skull (SKUL) The bones in an animal's head that protect its brain.

support (suh-PORT) To hold up.

tissues (TIH-shooz) Matter that forms the parts of living things.

vertebral column (ver-TEH-brel KAH-lum) The bones that run down a person's or animal's back and protect its spinal cord.

Index

B
ball-and-socket
    joint, 19
blood, 7, 22

C
carpus bones, 19
cartilage, 8, 16

F
femur, 20
fibula, 20

H
hinge joint(s), 11,
    19

humerus, 19

J
joint(s), 8, 11

M
metacarpus bones,
    19
movable joints, 11
muscles, 4, 15

P
phalanges, 19

S
saddle joints, 11

shoulder girdle, 16,
    19–20
skull, 11–12, 15
spinal cord, 15
spongy bone, 7
synovial membrane,
    8

T
tibia, 20

V
vertebrae, 15
vertebral column,
    11, 15–16

Web Sites

Due to the changing nature of Internet links, PowerKids Press has developed an online list of Web sites related to the subject of this book. This site is updated regularly. Please use this link to access the list:
www.powerkidslinks.com/hybw/skeletal/